DHS Headquarters Consolidation Project: Issues for Congress

William L. Painter

Analyst in Emergency Management and Homeland Security Policy

September 21, 2012

Congressional Research Service

7-5700

www.crs.gov

R42753

CRS Report for Congress

Prepared for Members and Committees of Congress

Summary

The Department of Homeland Security (DHS) was established in early 2003, bringing together existing parts of 22 different federal agencies and departments in a new framework of operations. In its first few years, the department was reorganized multiple times, and more focus was given to ensuring its components were addressing the perceived threats facing the country rather than to addressing the new organization's management structure and headquarters needs. Therefore, the consolidation of physical infrastructure that one might expect in creating an operation of such size and breadth did not occur.

As the Coast Guard began to plan consolidating its leases on headquarters facilities into secure federally owned space, DHS was finding its original headquarters space at the Nebraska Avenue Complex too limited to meet its evolving needs. In 2006, the George W. Bush Administration proposed combining the two projects into one $3.45 billion headquarters consolidation project on the West Campus of St. Elizabeths Hospital in Anacostia.

Since that year, Administrations of both parties have requested funding for this initiative. However, this project has not received sustained funding from Congress—over 80% of the funding it has received so far came in FY2009 when a surge of supplemental funding combined with the regular appropriations for the General Services Administration (GSA) and DHS provided almost $1.1 billion for the project. With the completion of its first key component (a new headquarters for the Coast Guard), this project faces an important turning point as budget pressures are impacting potential capital projects across the government and the Administration is developing a new construction plan and cost estimate for DHS headquarters in response.

The purpose of this report is to outline the policy considerations to be evaluated in deciding whether to continue funding the consolidated DHS headquarters at St. Elizabeths, and to explore some of the benefits and consequences of several possible ways forward.

The fate of this initiative could have significant impact on the department operationally, budgetarily, and culturally. Operationally, the consolidated headquarters would provide a higher level of security for many DHS headquarters functions, and would provide a more capable departmental operations center to help coordinate the federal response to natural disasters and terrorist attacks. Budgetarily, the department would benefit from reduced overhead costs in the long term, but would face significant pressure on its near term budget to see the construction through to completion. Culturally, the new headquarters could help promote the integration of the department's components into "One DHS," and have some direct and indirect contributions to improving departmental morale.

The report looks at five potential ways forward for the headquarters project: immediate termination of it and disposal of the site; moving the Coast Guard in but going no further; moving the Coast Guard in and proceeding with developing the departmental operations center complex and top management offices; rescoping the Coast Guard building as a smaller headquarters for the department overall; and aggressively funding the project to accelerate completion.

Whatever decision is made—even an option to not make a decision on the long-term fate of the project—will bear significant costs, manifested as a combination of up-front construction costs, ongoing lease expenses, and operational and management tradeoffs that are difficult to quantify.

This report will be updated as events warrant.

Contents

Figures

Tables

Appendixes

Contacts

Background

The Department of Homeland Security (DHS) was established by the Homeland Security Act of 2002 (P.L. 107-296, hereafter the HSA) and became operational January 24, 2003, barely sixteen months after the terrorist attacks on the Pentagon and World Trade Center on September 11, 2001. Rather than being as a completely new entity, the department was established by assembling existing parts of 22 different federal agencies and departments into a new framework.[1] The timing and means of establishing DHS, coupled with the perceived urgency of its mission in its early years, hastened the growth and development of the department's operational capabilities. At the same time, these factors hindered potential efforts to more fully integrate the functions of the department's different components.

The headquarters functions of the department's components were not physically consolidated at the time, but instead were left scattered across the National Capital Region in accordance with their past history, rather than their new role in the DHS. As a result, DHS today stands as the third-largest department of the federal government,[2] but runs its operations from about 50 different locations in the National Capital Region.

In 2004, the Coast Guard (one of the larger components of the newly-minted DHS) began to explore how to meet its needs for new headquarters facilities. The General Services Administration (GSA), the Office of Management and Budget (OMB), and DHS determined that a federally-owned site would be more cost-effective than securing a replacement lease. In the meantime, the current location of the DHS headquarters—a former Navy facility at the corner of Nebraska and Massachusetts Avenues in northwest Washington, DC (known as "the NAC"— short for "the Nebraska Avenue Complex")—was proving to be inadequate. One of the initial assumptions at the time of the establishment of DHS was that the department would only need a headquarters staff of roughly 800 persons. Once the department was established and roles, responsibilities, and management needs became clear, DHS determined that the NAC was inadequate to meet mission execution requirements.[3]

GSA had determined that the St. Elizabeths Hospital[4] site in Anacostia, which had recently been declared excess by the Department of Health and Human Services, was a potential site for federal agencies with high security requirements.

President George W. Bush's FY2006 budget request had announced the Administration's plan to consolidate the Coast Guard's headquarters on the West Campus of St. Elizabeths—an initiative that received initial funding in GSA's budget that year.[5] The Administration's FY2007 budget request sought the initial tranche of funding for the new Coast Guard headquarters through the DHS appropriations bill, but both House and Senate appropriators, when briefed on the idea of a larger consolidation project for DHS headquarters at the site, directed DHS to not proceed on either project until a new headquarters master plan was completed.[6]

---

[1] A complete list can be found at http://www.dhs.gov/xabout/history/editorial_0133.shtm.

[2] This relative ranking is based on the number of employees.

[3] CRS discussions with GSA and DHS staff during site visit to St. Elizabeths, November 16th, 2011.

[4] The formal name of the site is "St. Elizabeths Hospital," spelled without an apostrophe.

[5] U.S. General Services Administration, *FY 2006 Congressional Justifications*, Washington, DC, February, 2006.

[6] H.Rept. 109-699, p. 118-199.

In October 2006, DHS Secretary Michael Chertoff put forward a master plan for "unifying ... core headquarters facilities with those of our operating components," which essentially broadened the Coast Guard project to include the overall DHS headquarters consolidation as well, moving 14,000 of the 22,000 people that staff headquarters functions for the department and its components to St. Elizabeths.[7] Earlier that year, the White House issued a report entitled "The Federal Response to Katrina: Lessons Learned." While this report did not call for a consolidated DHS headquarters *per se*, it did state a need to develop a joint departmental operations center with robust command and control functions to promote more efficient incident response.[8] This need would be used to help advocate for the consolidated headquarters project in future years.

Since that year, Administrations of both parties have requested funding for this initiative to support a coordinated construction plan. However, this project has not received consistent funding—over 80% of the funding it has received so far came in FY2009 when a surge of supplemental funding combined with the regular appropriations for GSA and DHS provided almost $1.1 billion for the project.

Given this lack of consistent funding, Administration officials have indicated that the coordinated construction schedule is no longer feasible and will need to be revised for future phases of the project. The Obama Administration's FY2013 budget request seeks funding for operational transition costs associated with moving the Coast Guard into its newly constructed headquarters building on the West Campus of St. Elizabeths, and to build highway infrastructure to support its operation, but no funding for GSA construction of later phases. The Administration has indicated that they will present a revised construction schedule and cost estimate for the project in the FY2014 budget request, or earlier. The decision on FY2013 funding coupled with the Administration's new plan for consolidation presents a unique opportunity for Congress to make clear its long-term vision for the department's headquarters and DHS overall.

The fate of this initiative could have significant impact on the department operationally, budgetarily, and culturally. Operationally, the consolidated headquarters would provide a higher level of security for many DHS headquarters functions compared to their current locations, and would provide a more capable departmental operations center to help coordinate the federal response to natural disasters and terrorist attacks. Budgetarily, the department would benefit from reduced overhead costs in the long term, but would face significant pressure on its near term budget to see the construction through to completion. Culturally, the new headquarters could help promote the integration of the department's components into "One DHS,"[9] and have some direct and indirect contributions to improving departmental morale.

---

[7] Department of Homeland Security, *Department of Homeland Security National Capital Region Housing Master Plan: Building a Unified Department*, Washington, DC, October 2006, p. 2.

[8] The White House, *The Federal Response to Hurricane Katrina: Lessons Learned*, Washington, DC, February 23, 2006, p.91.

[9] "One DHS" is a term used by past and present secretaries of the department to describe a DHS that operates as a single unit rather than a collection of individual components.

Arguments for and Against Headquarters Consolidation

Justifications Made for Consolidation

The initial DHS National Capital Region Housing Master Plan stated that increased consolidation and co-location of DHS headquarters functions was needed to accomplish five objectives:

- Improve mission effectiveness;

- Create a unified DHS organization;

- Increase organizational efficiency;

- Adjust the size of the real estate portfolio to better fit the mission of DHS; and

- Reduce real estate occupancy costs.

In testimony before the House Appropriations Committee Homeland Security Subcommittee on March 25, 2010, Elaine Duke, Under Secretary for Management for the department, simplified this list to three reasons:

- To increase effectiveness and efficiency;

- To enhance communication; and

- To "foster a "one DHS" culture that would optimize department-wide, prevention, response and recovery capabilities."

Former DHS Secretary Michael Chertoff, who signed the original DHS Consolidation Master Plan, recently described the consolidation project as being "very important both from symbolic and operational standpoint. It would provide an enormous amount of leverage in defining the department."[10]

Many of DHS's components are in leased facilities, despite the fact that the government's existing policy is to use federally owned sites for national security functions.[11] Consolidation would help bring DHS in line with that policy, which would also reduce the department's overhead costs.

Why St. Elizabeths?

The DHS Housing Master Plan analyzed fifteen possible sites to see if they could meet the department's requirements. DHS and GSA determined in their program of requirements for DHS in the National Capital Region that DHS needed a minimum of 4.5 million square feet of office space specifically for headquarters functions on a secure campus, housing nearly 14,000 DHS

---

[10] Chertoff, Michael, response to question posed to a panel on "The Department of Homeland Security: Past, Present, and Future," at the Aspen Security Forum, July 28, 2012. Video available at http://aspensecurityforum.org/2012-video-day-3.

[11] General Services Administration, "DHS Headquarters Location Analysis," September, 2008, p. 6.

personnel, out of an overall need for 7.1 million square feet in the region.[12] The NAC, if fully developed, could only provide 1.2 million square feet.[13]

Aside from space, the other requirements noted in the study were:

- Compatibility with DHS security needs;
- Closeness to the White House and Congress;
- Availability for development by DHS;
- Ability to be ready on DHS's timetable;
- Proximity to major roadways;
- Proximity to mass transit;
- Proximity to neighborhood amenities; and
- Availability of an adjacent parcel that can accommodate additional office development and parking.

The analysis found St. Elizabeths was the best match, meeting eight of the nine requirements (neighborhood amenities were not deemed present at the time, but were anticipated to develop). According to GSA, St. Elizabeths was the only site available that was capable of meeting DHS's needs.[14]

In addition, under 41 CFR Section 102-73.255, "prior to acquiring, constructing, or leasing buildings (or sites for such buildings), Federal agencies must use, to the maximum extent feasible, historic properties available to the agency."[15]

Other benefits often cited for consolidation at the St. Elizabeths Campus include economic benefits to the local community and security benefits to nearby federal facilities. St. Elizabeths, since its establishment, has been a government-controlled closed campus. It overlooks Joint Base Anacostia-Bolling[16] and the Defense Information Systems Agency, which has expressed its desire that the property remain a government-controlled closed campus.

Concerns Voiced over Consolidation

Opponents of consolidation have questioned the need for a single large headquarters. Some critics have expressed the belief that the single headquarters concept is outdated, proposing "distributed" headquarters facilities connected via the Internet.[17] With new constraints on the DHS budget, the

---

[12] Department of Homeland Security, *Department of Homeland Security National Capital Region Housing Master Plan: Building a Unified Department*, Washington, DC, October 2006, p. 5.

[13] Ibid., p. 7.

[14] Department of Homeland Security, *Department of Homeland Security National Capital Region Housing Master Plan: Building a Unified Department*, Washington, DC, October 2006, pp. 4-5.

[15] 41 CFR 102-73.255, as downloaded from GPOAccess's "Electronic Code of Federal Regulations," http://ecfr.gpoaccess.gov.

[16] Former known as Bolling Air Force Base and the Anacostia Naval Annex.

[17] Slabbert, Nicholas, "Telecommunities," Urban Land Institute, May 2005. As downloaded from http://www.virtualadjacency.com/wp-content/uploads/2008/01/9-uli-telecommunities-may2005.pdf.

department's workforce is unlikely to meet growth projections that formed part of the justification for the project's size. Others oppose consolidation on the grounds that the department's establishment was flawed and that its overall structure should be revisited.[18]

As is noted in later sections of the report, concerns have been voiced by Members of Congress about schedule delays and cost increases.

Why Not St. Elizabeths?

Some historic preservationists voiced concerns that the project would fail to preserve the historic character of the site,[19] while others have balked at the cost of "constructive reuse" of the site's historic buildings. Some in the local community have questioned whether a secure campus like the envisioned DHS headquarters will support significant economic activity in the surrounding area.[20] According to GSA testimony in 2010, the project would create 30,000 direct and indirect jobs during construction.[21] As of July 2012, according to GSA's website for the project, 4,690 people have been employed by the project, including 717 District residents.[22]

As noted in later sections of the report, concerns have been voiced by Members of Congress about the operational impacts of the Coast Guard being the only part of DHS that moves to the site.

Funding History

Funding for civilian federal government facilities is often provided through two separate sources—through the GSA, which is funded in the Financial Services and General Government Appropriations bill, and through the appropriations bill that funds the agency that will use the facility. The construction of basic buildings in most cases is done through contracts let by and funded through GSA. The department that will use the building pays for "tenant improvements"—security, furniture, mission-specific equipment, amenities and other finishes that make the building functional for its occupants.

---

[18] O'Connell, Jonathan, "St. Elizabeths Renovation as Security Campus Faces Resistance," *The Washington Post*, March 30, 2012.

[19] Moe, Richard, "A Disaster for St. Elizabeths," *The Washington Post*, January 8, 2009.

[20] Sheridan, Mary Beth, "Scouting a New Home for Homeland Security," *The Washington Post*, October 14, 2007.

[21] Written testimony of Robert Peck, Commissioner, Public Buildings Service, General Services Administration, "Homeland Security Headquarters Facilities," before the House Appropriations Committee's Homeland Security Subcommittee, March 25, 2010. Available at http://www.gsa.gov/portal/content/104271.

[22] General Services Administration, *Opportunities Center Employment Summary*, available at http://stelizabethsdevelopment.com, as of viewed September 11, 2012.

Figure 1. GSA and DHS funding for DHS St. Elizabeths Headquarters, FY2006-2012

(millions of dollars of budget authority)

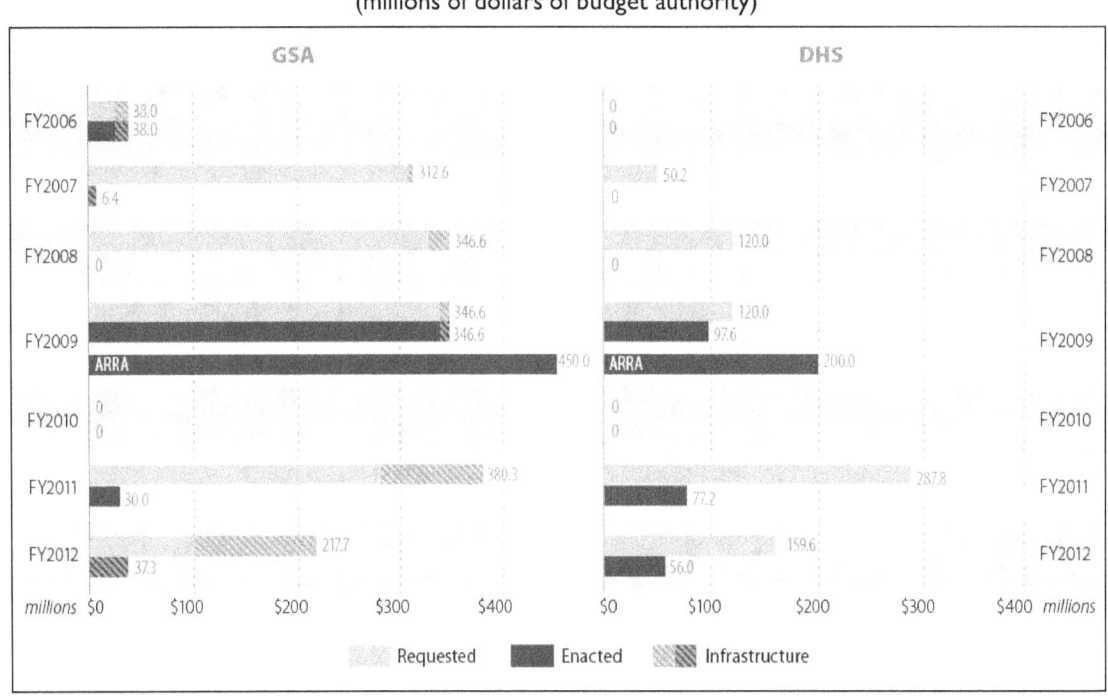

Source: FY2006-FY2012 conference reports and the U.S. General Services Administration's *FY2012 Expenditure Plan and Reprogramming Request for the Federal Buildings Fund.*

Note: Some of GSA's appropriations for St. Elizabeths pay for infrastructure and improvements that would be needed for any redevelopment of the site—a core responsibility of the GSA. As it could be argued that these costs therefore are not directly attributable to the DHS headquarters project, CRS has attempted to distinguish between the two. A detailed table of requests and appropriations is provided in the Appendix.

Figure 1 shows the funding requests made by previous and present Administrations through GSA and DHS for DHS headquarters consolidation at St. Elizabeths, including funding for infrastructure improvements at the site once the initial headquarters project was announced, and the appropriations provided by Congress in response, from FY2006 through FY2012.[23]

The St. Elizabeths project has to date received more than $1.3 billion in appropriations. The original cost estimate for the consolidation of DHS headquarters at St. Elizabeths was $3.4 billion.[24] According to DHS, all funded components of the project have proceeded on time and within their budget projections.[25] However, the project has not been consistently funded to the levels requested under Administrations of either party.

---

[23] GSA had a separate project to fund infrastructure upgrades at St. Elizabeths for future use, separate from the DHS headquarters consolidation project. However, as these upgrades support the headquarters consolidation, they are included to provide a more complete picture of the funding stream.

[24] Duke, Elaine C., DHS Under Secretary for Management, written testimony, "Homeland Security Headquarters Facilities," before the House Appropriations Committee Homeland Security Subcommittee, March 25, 2010, p. 11. Available at http://ipv6.dhs.gov/ynews/testimony/testimony_1274279995276.shtm.

[25] Borras, Rafael, DHS Under Secretary for Management, written testimony, "Department of Homeland Security Facilities Hearing," before the House Appropriations Committee Homeland Security Subcommittee, March 21, 2012. Available at http://www.dhs.gov/news/2012/03/29/written-testimony-under-secretary-management-rafael-borras-house-appropriations.

As the figure illustrates, requests for funding were made but not fulfilled for the larger consolidation project in FY2007 and FY2008, which slowed the start of the project. The original DHS National Capital Region Master Plan envisioned the Coast Guard moving into its new headquarters in the last quarter of FY2010—a move now slated for the second half of FY2013.[26]

FY2009 was the only year the St. Elizabeths project as presently envisioned received funding of more than $100 million from either the DHS or GSA budget. The first of two consolidated appropriations bills[27] included funding for the Department of Homeland Security, including $98 million for the Coast Guard Headquarters element of the project.[28] Five months later, outside the traditional allocation-constrained debate of regular appropriations bills, the American Recovery and Reinvestment Act of 2009[29] (ARRA) invested $650 million in this capital project.[30] The FY2009 regular appropriations process concluded about three weeks later with the second of the two consolidated appropriations bills,[31] which included $347 million for the project through GSA, matching the level requested by the Administration through the GSA budget request.[32]

Requests for funding in FY2011 and FY2012 were only partially met. As a result of these lower funding levels, the projected project completion date has slipped to the point that the coordinated construction plan—designed to maximize efficiency in construction by doing the work in large simultaneous phases—is being revisited, and a new cost estimate is being generated along with that plan.

Table A-1, which outlines the history of requests and appropriations for this project in detail is included in the appendix, as well as a summary of the appropriations provisions from the other years where funding was requested.

Current Status

Project Status

In the final consolidated appropriations bill for FY2012, the overall combined request of $377 million for GSA and DHS contributions to St. Elizabeths garnered $93 million in appropriations, with enough funding provided to DHS to complete only the construction of the Coast Guard portion of the headquarters.[33] GSA provided $37 million out of the $50 million it received for construction projects nationwide.

---

[26] Department of Homeland Security, *Department of Homeland Security National Capital Region Housing Master Plan: Building a Unified Department*, Washington, DC, October 2006, p.16.

[27] P.L. 110-329, 122 Stat. 3574.

[28] House Appropriations Committee Print, *Consolidated Security, Disaster Assistance, and Continuing Appropriations Act, 2009* (P.L. 110-329), *Division D—Department of Homeland Security Appropriations Act, 2009*, p. 589.

[29] P.L. 111-5, 123 Stat. 115.

[30] H.Rept. 111-16, p. 48, 432. ARRA was an economic stimulus package that provided almost $800 billion in appropriations and revenue provisions passed in the midst of a recession.

[31] P.L. 111-8, 123 Stat. 524.

[32] House Appropriations Committee Print, *Omnibus Appropriations Act, 2009* (P.L. 111-8), *Division D—Financial Services and General Government Appropriations Act, 2009*, p. 907.

[33] In their spending plan released on January 27, 2012, GSA indicated they would spend $37 million on the St. Elizabeths project.

Discussions with DHS officials and testimony before Congress have indicated DHS is preparing a new approach to the St. Elizabeths project in light of the limitations on available funding. The original plan for St. Elizabeths was a coordinated approach, intended to maximize cost savings by coordinating construction efforts across the campus. DHS has indicated that continuing with the original integrated construction plan given the level of appropriations in FY2011 and FY2012 (which would not be feasible due to the level of appropriations required in individual future years) would stretch the timeline for project completion to FY2022 and raise the estimated overall cost to $4 billion.[34] DHS Under Secretary for Management Rafael Borras noted in testimony before the House Appropriations Committee's Homeland Security subcommittee that future requests would be scoped and packaged as individual segments rather than as larger coordinated pieces.[35]

CRS has made inquiries with DHS regarding revisions to the schedule and cost estimates for the project. The department indicated that no additional information had been approved for release beyond the information provided in the FY2013 budget request.[36] The budget request indicates DHS has funding to complete the first phase of the project, including the Coast Guard Headquarters, perimeter security and utilities to support the headquarters, and adaptive reuse of six historic buildings to support the Coast Guard presence.[37] However, briefing materials provided by DHS indicate that GSA did not receive the minimum required funding for completing its first phase requirements,[38] and they have had to delay several items in Phase I that are not critical to Coast Guard occupancy. These will have to be completed later at higher cost, but redirecting that funding will allow the Coast Guard headquarters part of the project to go ahead.[39]

The original plans called for a consolidated departmental operations center to be excavated and built at the same time as the Coast Guard headquarters. As the Coast Guard headquarters building was built into the side of a hill, the original construction plan would have taken advantage of the availability of the specialized crew and open space created by the construction to facilitate development of this new facility. Funding was not provided for this work, however, so this piece of the project will have to be developed at a later date and most likely at a higher cost, according to DHS and GSA. Should Congress fund the provide the necessary operational transition costs for the Coast Guard to move to St. Elizabeths in FY2013, the operations center for the Coast Guard and campus security control center will occupy some of the available space.[40]

Aside from individual cases like the one noted above in which efficiencies from concurrent construction will not be realized, delays in construction are projected to result in other cost increases. According to Borras, "It is expected that future construction work will increase in cost

---

[34] E-mail to CRS from DHS Legislative Affairs, September 4, 2012.

[35] Rafael Borras, response to questioning during "Department of Homeland Security Facilities Hearing," before the House Appropriations Committee Homeland Security Subcommittee, March 21, 2012.

[36] Author telephone conversation with DHS officials, August 7, 2012.

[37] U.S. Department of Homeland Security, *Fiscal Year 2013 Congressional Justification*, Departmental Management and Operations, DHS Headquarters Consolidation Project, Washington, DC, February 13, 2012, p. 4.

[38] According to DHS, GSA needed $76 million to complete all activities associated with Phase I of the project, which generally encompassed the Coast Guard headquarters and groundwork for the rest of the consolidated headquarters campus.

[39] U.S. Department of Homeland Security, *DHS Headquarters Consolidation Congressional Staff Tour/Update*, July 27, 2012, p. 4.

[40] Author's conversations with DHS and GSA officials, November 16, 2011.

---

due to current industry escalation standards, which indicate annual increases between 5 and 12 percent through 2017."[41]

FY2013 Appropriations

The Administration's FY2013 budget request for the Department of Homeland Security includes $89 million for construction related to St. Elizabeths, and $24.5 million for the Coast Guard to cover operational transition costs for the move to the new facility. The GSA budget includes no funding request for the project. However, it is noteworthy that the DHS budget justification indicated the request is "to construct I-295/Malcolm X Avenue interchange improvements and West Campus access road extension from Gate 4 of the U. S. Coast Guard Headquarters Building to Malcolm X Avenue."[42] Funding for this type of infrastructure, which in this case supports access to multiple federal facilities aside from the St. Elizabeths campus, has traditionally been requested and provided in the GSA budget.

The House Appropriations Committee recommended no funding for the highway interchange or any part of the St. Elizabeths project through the management accounts, noting in its report the irregularity of funding a highway interchange through the Homeland Security bill. The bill does provide the Administration's requested funding for the Coast Guard. In addition, $10 million is provided through the Coast Guard's construction budget to provide additional support for the project.

In the report accompanying H.R. 5855, the committee noted the following:

> The Committee recommends no new construction funding in the bill for new Departmental Headquarters Consolidation expansion. This is $89,000,000 below the request. Funding is included, as requested, as part of the Coast Guard appropriation to cover the costs associated with completing the move of the Coast Guard headquarters to St. Elizabeths. Associated with this, as described below, is additional funding under Coast Guard construction to ensure completion of the current project, improve site access, and support analysis for follow on work and any necessary planning adjustments for schedule, scope, and cost.
>
> ...
>
> The Committee understands that the Department ... is actively exploring options to creatively modify or consolidate current leases, in the expectation that a permanent headquarters construction site will be significantly delayed or amended. The Committee encourages the Department to continue this effort and to inform the Committee of its progress in consolidation no later than 90 days after the date of enactment of this Act, including a revised schedule and cost estimates. Further, as noted above, the Committee includes $10,000,000 under the Coast Guard Acquisition, Construction, and Improvements account to complete Phase 1 of construction, ensure Coast Guard will be able to move in

---

[41] Borras, Rafael, DHS Under Secretary for Management, written testimony, "Department of Homeland Security Facilities Hearing," before the House Appropriations Committee Homeland Security Subcommittee, March 21, 2012. Available at http://www.dhs.gov/news/2012/03/29/written-testimony-under-secretary-management-rafael-borras-house-appropriations.

[42] U.S. Department of Homeland Security, *Fiscal Year 2013 Congressional Justification*, Departmental Management and Operations, DHS Headquarters Consolidation Project, Washington, DC, February 13, 2012, p. 5.

2013 and that there will be no obstacles to access and transportation into the site, and to support orderly planning and analysis for the overall project.[43]

In the minority views accompanying the report, the ranking members of the subcommittee and full committee noted the following:

> The bill also fails to provide the $89 million for site access, including necessary road and interchange improvements, for DHS personnel to access the new DHS headquarters. The new DHS headquarters project has been shortchanged over the past few years, causing repeated schedule delays and increasing the costs from $3.4 billion to just over $4 billion if all three phases are constructed. In the interim, the Coast Guard may be the only tenant at this new facility for the next 3-5 years, as the bill funds only this relocation in 2013. The bill does not include any funding for Phase 2, which was to begin construction for DHS central headquarters and FEMA.[44]

The Senate Appropriations Committee recommended $89 million for the highway interchange, although it was funded as a part of the Under Secretary for Management's office through a general provision rather than as a stand-alone appropriation in departmental operations as requested. The committee also fully funded the Coast Guard's operational transition costs for the move. No funding was provided for the project through the Coast Guard construction budget. An amendment[45] was offered in full committee markup on May 22, 2012, to use the $89 million for the highway interchange as an offset for an unrelated amendment. The amendment failed on a 15-15 vote, and the funding remains in the reported version of the legislation.

In the report accompanying S. 3216, the committee noted the following:

> Pursuant to section 549, a total of $89,000,000 is provided for "Office of the Under Secretary for Management" for costs associated with headquarters consolidation and mission support consolidation. The Under Secretary shall submit an expenditure plan no later than 90 days after the date of enactment of this act detailing how these funds will be allocated, including a revised schedule and cost estimates for headquarters consolidation. Quarterly briefings are required on headquarters and mission support consolidation activities, including any deviation from the expenditure plan. According to the Department, an updated plan is being developed in coordination with the General Services Administration to complete the headquarters consolidation project in smaller, independent segments that are more fiscally manageable in the current budget environment. The Department expects this updated plan to be completed by the end of summer 2012 and it is to be submitted to the Committee upon its completion. The Committee expects the plan to identify the discrete construction segments, the associated resource requirements for each segment, and the proposed timeline for requesting funding to complete each segment.[46]

Other Congressional Action

During its hearings on the FY2013 budget request the House Appropriations Committee's Homeland Security Subcommittee held a hearing on DHS facilities, focusing on two major DHS construction projects for which funding has been sought in recent years with limited success: the

---

[43] H.Rept. 112-492, pp. 19-20.

[44] H.Rept. 112-492, p. 204.

[45] Senator Dan Coats and Senator Kay Bailey Hutchison

[46] S.Rept. 112-169, p. 20.

consolidated headquarters project and the National Bio- and Agro-defense Facility. Subcommittee Chairman Robert Aderholt pointed out that both projects "are complex and expensive undertakings with multi-year timelines," and "are also operating under significantly tighter budgets than anticipated when planning began several years ago." He went on to say that Congress "must take a more realistic look at [the St. Elizabeths project] and balance delays against possible cost increases," while asking DHS for minimum funding requirements and alternative solutions.[47]

Prior to the completion of the FY2012 appropriations process, on September 23, 2011, the House Committee Transportation and Infrastructure's Subcommittee on Coast Guard and Maritime Transportation held a hearing to review the status of the DHS headquarters consolidation project, focusing on the move of the Coast Guard to the new location, and the effect it would have on the Coast Guard's budget and operations. The subcommittee chairman noted that in 2006, the Coast Guard authorization bill required GSA to provide in its master plan for another agency of DHS to move to St. Elizabeths at about the same time. This was done out of concern that the Coast Guard would be "isolated" at the Anacostia site, both in the sense of continuing the pattern of fragmentation of DHS component headquarters, and the lack of needed road infrastructure to access the site, which he noted was a long-standing concern of the subcommittee.[48] The subcommittee ranking member noted that "No one's questioned the need to complete the consolidation. For that matter, no one…has seriously proposed its termination." He went on to say that not funding the project would lead to "a DHS that is less efficient, less coordinated and less effective than it could be if this project was successfully completed."[49]

S. 1546, the Department of Homeland Security Authorization Act of 2011, which was marked up by the Senate Homeland Security and Governmental Affairs Committee on September 21, 2011, included a section on DHS headquarters consolidation, directing that DHS consolidate its headquarters function at St. Elizabeths no later than the end of FY2018, and that all remaining departmental components and activities that be consolidated "to as few locations within the National Capitol [sic] Region as possible."[50]

There is a comparatively high volume of commentary on the legislative record regarding the DHS headquarters consolidation project from the appropriations committees relative to the authorizing committees and individual members. The appropriators generally respond to the Administration's annual requests for funding in a specific fashion and often with an explanation of their position, and therefore touch on most topics that have funding needs associated with them on an annual basis. The authorizers do not necessarily present legislation and accompanying reports on a specific topic like this each year, and floor time dedicated to this particular issue has been limited. Members of the House and Senate have a variety of ways to express their position on a particular issue, many of which are not readily available for analysis. Therefore, an absence of on-the-

---

[47] Representative Robert Aderholt, opening statement to "Department of Homeland Security Facilities Hearing," before the House Appropriations Committee Homeland Security Subcommittee, March 21, 2012.

[48] Representative Frank LoBiondo, opening statement to "Review and Status of the Multibillion-Dollar Department of Homeland Security Relocation Project in Washington, DC, and its Impacts on the U.S. Coast Guard," House Transportation and Infrastructure Subcommittee on Coast Guard and Maritime Transportation, September 23, 2011, p. 1.

[49] Rep. Rick Larsen, opening statement to "Review and Status of the Multibillion-Dollar Department of Homeland Security Relocation Project in Washington, DC, and its Impacts on the U.S. Coast Guard," House Transportation and Infrastructure Subcommittee on Coast Guard and Maritime Transportation, September 23, 2011, p. 3.

[50] Sec. 211, S. 1546.

---

record commentary does not necessarily reflect the degree of concern with, support for, or opposition to the project.

Considerations for Congress

Implications of the Consolidated Headquarters Project

Consolidating DHS headquarters anywhere would change the department's current operating patterns in the National Capital Region. These changes would have operational, budgetary and cultural implications for DHS, and the consolidation vision presented in the St. Elizabeths project would provide its own particular texture to these changes.

Operations

Consolidating the headquarters components of DHS at a single site would facilitate both "vertical" coordination between departmental and component leadership and "horizontal" coordination among the department's components. With headquarters functions operating in spaces designed for a unified department, the structural hurdles to coordination are lowered. Having a single campus makes collaboration with other components easier to accomplish and can facilitate more effective departmental leadership.

The lack of a consolidated headquarters has hindered the development of a cohesive, maximally effective department in the eyes of some observers close to DHS.[51] Former Coast Guard Commandant Thad Allen testified on July 12, 2012 before the Senate Committee on Homeland Security and Governmental Affairs:

> In the Washington Area the Department remains a disjointed collection of facilities and the future of the relocation to the St. Elizabeths campus remains in serious doubt. One of the great opportunity costs that will occur if this does not happen will be the failure to create a fully functioning National Operations Center for the Department that could serve as the integrating node for departmental wide operations and establish the competency and credibility of the Department to coordinate homeland security related events and responses across government as envisioned by the Homeland Security Act. As with the mission support functions discussed earlier, the Department has struggled to evolve an operational planning and mission execution coordination capability. As a result, the most robust command and control functions and capabilities in the Department reside at the component level...
>
> The combination of these factors, in my view, has severely constrained the ability [of] the Department [to] mature as an enterprise. And while there is significant potential for increased efficiencies and effectiveness, the real cause for action remains the creation of unity of effort that enables better mission performance. In this regard, there is no higher

---

[51] For example, Rep. Bennie Thompson, opening statement to "Consolidating DHS: An Update on the St. Elizabeths Project," hearing before the Subcommittee on Management, Investigations, and Oversight of the Committee on Homeland Security, House of Representatives, March 26, 2009, available at https://www.hsdl.org/?view&did=25147; and Chertoff, Michael, "The Department of Homeland Security: Past, Present, and Future," at the Aspen Security Forum, July 28, 2012. Video available at http://aspensecurityforum.org/2012-video-day-3.

priority than removing barriers to information sharing within the department and improved operational planning and execution.[52]

National Operations Center

Currently, DHS operates a National Operations Center (NOC) at the Nebraska Avenue Complex. However, its ability to provide a robust command and control function and coordinate federal government incident response to an incident is constrained by its limited size and infrastructure.

Establishment of the type of NOC described in Admiral Allen's testimony would have direct impact on both day-to-day and crisis operations of the department. Establishment of a new NOC was recommended in *The Federal Response to Katrina: Lessons Learned*, the White House's extensive after-action report from the hurricanes that hit the Gulf Coast in 2005. The report's specific recommendation is as follows:

> In order to strengthen DHS's operational management capabilities, we must structure the Department's headquarters elements to support the Secretary's incident management responsibilities. First and most important, Federal government response organizations must be co-located and strengthened to manage catastrophes in a new National Operations Center (NOC). The mission of the NOC must be to coordinate and integrate the national response and provide a common operating picture for the entire Federal government.[53]

In addition, under the plan for the consolidated headquarters, the new NOC would be co-located with the operations centers of the individual DHS components. In *Homeland Security: Opportunities Exist to Enhance Collaboration at 24/7 Operations Centers Staffed by Multiple DHS Agencies*, GAO agreed that DHS's plans to co-locate its headquarters, its component headquarters and their respective staffs and operations centers at one location "could further enhance collaboration among DHS's component agencies," along with adoption of other key practices.[54] DHS has further indicated that increased operational effectiveness would result from the co-location of operations centers, and real estate efficiencies could be found from shared common functions, support rooms, and incident management spaces.[55]

The establishment of a new, more capable NOC without the presence of a consolidated headquarters would be difficult. The consolidated headquarters project brings, for the first time, the executive leadership of the department and a leadership presence from all its components together. Without consolidation, the NOC would necessarily be separated from either the executive levels of DHS or the leadership of components implementing the response.

---

[52] Statement of Thad W. Allen, Admiral, U.S. Coast Guard (retired), "The Future of Homeland Security: The Evolution of the Homeland Security Department's Roles and Missions," Senate Committee on Homeland Security and Government Affairs, 112th Cong., 1st sess., July 12, 2012. Available at http://www.hsgac.senate.gov/hearings/the-future-of-homeland-security-the-evolution-of-the-homeland-security-departments-roles-and-missions.

[53] The White House, *The Federal Response to Katrina: Lessons Learned*, Washington, DC, 2006, pp. 69-70.

[54] GAO-07-89, *Homeland Security: Opportunities Exist to Enhance Collaboration at 24/7 Operations Centers Staffed by Multiple DHS Agencies*, October 2006, p. 8.

[55] E-mail from DHS Legislative Affairs, September 4, 2012. Available from author on request.

Physical Facility Security

One operational question that arises in relation to this project is the advisability of a consolidated headquarters capacity from a security standpoint. Does consolidating the leadership of DHS at a single facility make it easier to secure, a more appealing target for efforts to disrupt it, or both?

In 1995, the Interagency Security Committee (ISC) was established by Executive Order 12977, and tasked with establishing policies for security of federal facilities, including developing and evaluating security standards. In 2003, it became part of DHS.

There are five levels of security standards for federal office buildings. Under the standards developed by the ISC, the proposed consolidated DHS headquarters would be classified as a Level V facility, the highest level on the scale. Buildings at this level are similar to those at the next level below in that they occupy more than 150,000 square feet and host more than 450 employees. The distinguishing characteristics of Level V facilities are that their missions "are considered critical to national security," and the buildings themselves are "high threat/high profile facilities."[56]

While the operators of Level V facilities customize their facility security to meet their mission needs, minimum standards for this type of facility include 100-foot perimeter setbacks, 100-foot separation between parking facilities and buildings, and protected ventilation equipment (located away from high-risk areas) for the buildings.[57] It is impossible for DHS to ensure this level of security for all its headquarters components in its current state of dispersal across the National Capital Region. The status quo would leave parts of the headquarters function in facilities that do not meet Level V security standards. While the Nebraska Avenue Complex (NAC), where the Secretary's Office is currently located provides Level V security,[58] it is too small to accommodate the needs of a consolidated headquarters outlined in the master plan.

Planning documents indicate that part of the reasoning behind the selection of the St. Elizabeths site was the ability to implement Level V security standards at this particular location.[59] The St. Elizabeths site was the only site in the District able to accommodate the office space requirement and the security standards.[60]

The security question extends beyond DHS headquarters' offices. These offices, for the most part, do not have the same level of security as the NAC, and often occupy leased office space in commercial buildings. If they are targeted by terrorist violence, it is likely neighboring offices, buildings and their personnel could be affected.

CIA headquarters and the Pentagon are high profile, consolidated headquarters that are considered Level V facilities. Both have been the targets of terrorist attacks. In the cases of attacks on both facilities, collateral damage was limited. If attacks using similar methodologies were carried out against DHS headquarters functions in their current locations, collateral damage

---

[56] GSA, "DHS Headquarters Consolidation Location Analysis," September 2008, pp. 9-10.

[57] Ibid, pp. 11-12.

[58] E-mail from DHS Legislative Affairs, August 8, 2012.

[59] In a side note, according to briefings by DHS officials, use of the site by DHS also will also contribute to the security of government communications and military facilities that the site overlooks.

[60] Ibid, p. 15-63.

would likely be greater due to the lack of separation of the DHS elements from the general population. For example, in February, 2010, a man flew a private plane into a commercial office building housing IRS offices in leased space. While the IRS was his intended target, the crash and fire affected other tenants in the building, including multiple non-federal businesses.[61]

It is also worth noting that both Level V facilities continued to operate in the face of the attacks. It is unlikely that targeted DHS offices with lower levels of security would be able to do the same.

One question would then seem to be, as there is already a Level V facility for part of DHS headquarters, does consolidating the headquarters function at St. Elizabeths further raise the profile of DHS, and make it a more likely target? This seems unlikely—DHS is already the third largest component of the federal government and is a well-known entity domestically and overseas. While the new headquarters would be larger, and parts are visible from a distance, it can be argued that the facility is no more intrusive than other defense-related facilities along the Potomac and Anacostia, the campus benefits from a significant setback, and the campus may be deemed a harder target than DHS's existing facilities as it was planned and built with DHS's needs in mind.

Regardless of whether the department's profile would be higher at St. Elizabeths, the essential question is whether whatever additional security risk that is entailed by consolidation is counterbalanced by whatever other operational, budgetary and cultural benefits may accrue, including the additional protection afforded headquarters elements currently outside the NAC that move to the new facility.

Budget

Priorities

In previous years, the St. Elizabeths project was treated as a high priority for the Administration. However, the last time current DHS Secretary Janet Napolitano mentioned headquarters consolidation in testimony for Congress was before the Senate Homeland Security and Governmental Affairs Committee on February, 2011, when she testified that the department "propose[d] to delay construction of the Federal Emergency Management Agency (FEMA) headquarters at St. Elizabeths as well as the deferral of other office co-locations, and building maintenance and enhancements to prioritize frontline security operations."[62] While a lower public profile for the project might be considered simply a change in legislative tactics, in September 2011, as Congress was working on the FY2012 appropriations bills, Secretary Napolitano said:

> With respect to DHS, yes, I expect we will flatten out and that's—that's not surprising. I mean, at the beginning of a department, of course you're going to be putting in more and more money until you get things kind of established and set up. There are things we'd like to do that are going to have to be postponed. St. Elizabeths is a good example, that's supposed to be our headquarters. We will have to postpone that... I'd rather have the money to

---

[61] Furness, Ashley and Jacob Dirr, "City and County Dedicate Web Site to Austin Plane Crash," February 18, 2010. http://www.bizjournals.com/austin/stories/2010/02/15/daily41 html?page=all

[62] Statement of The Honorable Janet Napolitano, Secretary, United States Department of Homeland Security, "The Homeland Security Department's Budget Submission for Fiscal Year 2012," Senate Committee on Homeland Security and Governmental Affairs, 112th Cong., 1st sess., February 17, 2011.

complete building a National Security Cutter for the Coast Guard and support the Secret Service in its activities, and sustain our efforts at the border [rather] than [have] a new building, and so that is why St. Es is on the chopping block for now. I think ultimately it will happen, but not now.[63]

The DHS Chief Financial Officer released the following statement shortly thereafter:

> The Secretary's comments that the DHS Headquarters Consolidation Project [is] on the "budget chopping block" was in context of a conversation on how congressional budget cuts are impacting the Department. The Administration is committed to building a new headquarters for the Department in DC and will continue to work with Congress to move this project forward while maintaining frontline operations. However, we are revisiting the original assumptions on the use of the space as St. Elizabeth's [sic] based on projected budgets and growth of the Department.[64]

As the Secretary alludes to in the former statement, the headquarters consolidation project was conceived in a different budget environment than exists today. At the time, projections for future budgets could have more easily accommodated such a significant capital investment. The DHS budget grew every year from the establishment of the department until it peaked in FY2010.

In the future fiscal environment influenced by the Budget Control Act[65] (BCA), it is reasonable to expect that the DHS budget will either remain relatively flat in nominal terms, or decline over the near future. The Administration's budget projections for the Department of Homeland Security through FY2018 show an increase of $3.2 billion—barely 8%—over six years. While the projections in the Administration's budget request are not binding, the minimal increases projected for FY2014-2018 indicate that a significant expansion in available budgetary resources is not anticipated.[66]

This project is significantly affected not only by the DHS budget, but the GSA's budget as well. Over $2 billion of the initially projected $3.4 billion in project costs was to be borne by the GSA through their budget.[67] However, as shown in **Figure 1**, as with DHS appropriations, GSA appropriations have not kept pace with the construction plan for the project. GSA's budget faces similar constraints as that of DHS. The amount appropriated for construction and acquisition of facilities has declined from nearly $894 million in FY2010 to $50 million in FY2012.[68] The fallout from recent scandals over inappropriate use of taxpayer funds at GSA could make

---

[63] Secretary of Homeland Security Janet Napolitano, press briefing, September 8, 2011, as recorded by Jason Miller of Federal News Radio and provided to CRS. Partial quote available in Jason Miller and Julia Ziegler's article, "DHS St. E's to be Victim of Budget Axe," FederalNewsRadio.com, September 9, 2011. http://www.federalnewsradio.com/?nid=741&sid=2534819

[64] Staff memorandum to Members of the House Committee on Transportation and Infrastructure Subcommittee on Coast Guard and Maritime Transportation, in re: Hearing on "Review and Status of the Multibillion-Dollar Department of Homeland Security Relocation Project in Washington, DC, and its Impacts on the U.S. Coast Guard," dated September 16, 2011.

[65] P.L. 112-25, 125 Stat. 240.

[66] *Budget of the United States Government, Fiscal Year 2013*, p. 240.

[67] Oral testimony of Robert Peck, Commissioner, Public Buildings Service, General Services Administration, "Homeland Security Headquarters Facilities," before the House Appropriations Committee's Homeland Security Subcommittee, March 25, 2010.

[68] CRS Report R40801, *Financial Services and General Government (FSGG): FY2010 Appropriations*, coordinated by Garrett Hatch, and CRS Report R42008, *Financial Services and General Government: FY2012 Appropriations*, coordinated by Garrett Hatch, p. 63.

---

increases to GSA's budget politically unpalatable, and the growing backlog of construction needs could create more competition for GSA's limited construction budget.

Even in this environment of fiscal constraint, however, Congress and the Administration continue to make affirmative choices to invest in a range of projects and services. The projected costs for DHS headquarters at St. Elizabeths could be met within the bounds of a BCA-influenced budget, or even a more limited one—the operative question is what level of priority is placed on this project in the overall budget by the Administration and, ultimately, by Congress. This prioritization could change significantly should the country be faced with another Katrina-scale incident where the lack of a more capable department-level operations center appears to constrain an effective federal response.

Overhead Savings

GSA and DHS have in previous years cited an estimated cost savings of $600 million over 30 years for the St. Elizabeths project. With the delays and cost increases described by Under Secretary Borras, these numbers would need to be revised based on the Administration's new timetable and segmented approach if it is approved.

Generally speaking, government agencies pay lease costs to the GSA or private real estate owners for the facilities they operate from. Reducing these costs by moving from leased properties to government-owned facilities can free up additional resources, alleviating pressure from declining agency budgets over the long term. The up-front costs of these projects in times of tightening budgets can be difficult for agencies to absorb in formulating their budget requests or for Congress to approve in the context of balancing other priorities, as the appropriations process makes no accounting for longer term savings.

As DHS has been attempting to consolidate its headquarters functions and other offices, its components that occupy leased space have faced another complicating factor. In testimony before the House Appropriations Committee's Homeland Security subcommittee, DHS noted that they currently have 181 leases in 53 locations for headquarters components, 87% of which expire by 2016.[69] As their leases have matured, they have added short term extensions so they can move to the envisioned new facilities or to space freed up by the movement of other offices. Delays in the completion of new space requires these offices to use more short term leases, which are more expensive, and thus raise the department's overhead costs.[70] With budgeting tending toward an environment where absorbing rising costs requires matching reductions in spending elsewhere, this could in turn, reduce the funding available for front line operations.

Aside from savings from lower leasing costs, some savings are to be expected with a consolidated headquarters from increased centralization of some support services. This should not be confused with the benefits of a "shared services" model for supporting the department or federal government. The use of shared services can generate efficiencies as well, but generally involves

---

[69] DHS handout, "Schedule Impacts to Migration Plan," distributed at "Department of Homeland Security Facilities Hearing," House Appropriations Committee Homeland Security Subcommittee, March 21, 2012.

[70] Oral testimony of Robert Peck, Commissioner, Public Buildings Service, General Services Administration, "Homeland Security Headquarters Facilities," before the House Appropriations Committee Homeland Security Subcommittee, March 25, 2010.

developing a different internal managerial relationship between enterprise operations and support functions, rather than simply consolidating them.[71]

Culture

"One DHS"

One common line of thought among secretaries of the department from the very beginning has been the need to fuse the diverse components of the department into a single unit—development of "one DHS."[72] However, the department has yet to accomplish this goal. As retired Coast Guard Commandant Admiral Thad Allen testified before the Senate Homeland Security and Governmental Affairs Committee, "There has been hesitancy by components to relinquish control and resources to a Department that appears to be still a work in progress."[73]

The question of whether the Department of Homeland Security should exist is not currently the focus of congressional debate. Although no authorization bill for the entire department has passed either chamber since the department was established, it is also true that no legislation to fundamentally alter the structure of DHS has been marked up since December, 2010.[74] Current issues include defining and refining the department's mission, and ensuring that the department can perform these missions effectively and efficiently. However, the persistence of some components' organizational structures from the pre-DHS era, the lack of integration between components with similar missions, and statements by prominent political figures[75] suggest that the issue is not completely settled.

Completion of a consolidated headquarters and co-location of headquarters functions is not sufficient to create the unified department with strong integrated management capacity across its components that is sought by Congress and the Administration. A repeated theme found in GAO analyses and in observations of witnesses testifying before the department's oversight committees is that successful integration of the department will take a long time to accomplish and require ongoing effort to maintain once it is achieved. Cathleen Berrick, in her capacity as Managing Director for Homeland Security and Justice Issues for the Government Accountability Office (GAO) had this to say in testimony before Congress on this particular challenge:

> In 2003, we designated the implementation and transformation of DHS as high risk because it represented an enormous and complex undertaking that would require time to achieve in an effective and efficient manner, and it has remained on our high-risk list since. We reported that the components that became part of DHS already faced a wide array of existing challenges, and any failure to effectively carry out the department's mission would expose

---

[71] Accenture, "Beyond Centralization: Deriving High Performance Through Fully Realized Shared Services," 2007, p. 5.

[72] Booz Allen Hamilton and Partnership for Public Service, "Securing the Future: Management Lessons of 9/11," August, 2011, p. 7.

[73] ADM Thad W. Allen, USCG (ret.), written testimony before the Senate Committee on Homeland Security and Governmental Affairs, "The Future of Homeland Security: The Evolution of the Homeland Security Department's Roles and Missions," July 12, 2012, p. 7.

[74] CRS analysis of Legislative Information System data as of September 18, 2012.

[75] Lee, Tony, "Gingrich Hopes New Contract Will Re-Energize Campaign," *Human Events*, October 3, 2011, p. 10. Laing, Keith, "George McGovern calls for eliminating TSA, Homeland Security," *The Hill*, November 17, 2011.

---

the nation to potentially serious consequences. In designating the implementation and transformation of DHS as high risk, we noted that building an effective department would require consistent and sustained leadership from top management to ensure the transformation of disparate agencies, program, and mission into an integrated organization, among other needs. Our prior work on mergers and acquisitions, undertaken before the creation of DHS, found that successful transformations of large organizations, even those faced with less strenuous reorganizations than DHS, can take years to achieve.[76]

The departmental leadership is aware of this challenge. Speaking at a hearing before the Senate Judiciary Committee, Secretary Napolitano noted:

> We continue to excavate differences in systems and cultures and protocols and procedures. There has been a lot accomplished over the past nine years by my two predecessors, and over the past three-plus years now that I've been Secretary.

> But given the size and scope of the merger that is underway, it does take time. The Department of Defense took, by most accounts, 40 years to really become unified as a department. My goal is to substantially beat that record.[77]

Consolidation of headquarters functions can contribute to this effort, and some observers believe it is a necessary step, but it is no "magic bullet" for the issues facing the department. The Department as recently as 2011 viewed consolidation of DHS headquarters operations as only one of seven key initiatives to integrate its management functions.[78]

Morale

Morale issues at DHS have been a matter of concern for both congressional authorizers and appropriators. Some observers have commented that DHS's low employee morale could be exacerbated by the lack of a unified organizational culture, one of the problems a consolidated headquarters was intended to address.

The most recent documentation of the comparatively low morale at the department can be found in the Partnership for Public Service's "Best Places to Work in the Federal Government"[79] analysis based on questions from the Office of Personnel Management's FedView survey of federal employees. There was no data reported from the OPM survey[80] to either directly confirm or refute the idea that headquarters consolidation would have an impact on morale. In fact, the issue of the adequacy of departmental facilities was not directly raised in the survey questions.

However, attitudes of DHS component staff reflected in several questions from the FedView survey could be reasonably expected to be impacted by the projected benefits of a consolidated

[76] Statement of Cathleen Berrick before the Subcommittee on Oversight of Government Management, the Federal Workforce, and the District of Columbia, U.S. Senate Committee on Homeland Security and Governmental Affairs, September, 30, 2010 (GAO-10-911T), pp. 1-2

[77] Napolitano, Janet, response to question, "Oversight of the Department of Homeland Security" Senate Judiciary Committee, April 25, 2012.

[78] GAO Report GAO-11-278, pp. 93-94.

[79] http://bestplacestowork.org/BPTW/rankings/

[80] United States Office of Personnel Management, *2011 Federal Employee Viewpoint Survey: Empowering Employees, Inspiring Change*, Washington, DC, September 22, 2011, pp. 35-38, http://www.fedview.opm.gov.

headquarters. For example, for those relocating to St. Elizabeths, the new headquarters is designed to include daycare facilities. This could be expected to improve the department's bottom-ranking scores linked to family-friendly culture and benefits among that group of employees. It is also possible that existence of a consolidated headquarters could change perceptions or performance of leadership more broadly across the department. However, issues of pay, advancement, diversity and matching employee skills to their missions would likely remain unaffected.[81]

Congressional decisions on capital investments in the department such as headquarters consolidation could be perceived by the employee base as an indirect validation or criticism of the department's work by Congress, or as a measure of the effectiveness of the departmental leadership in representing DHS interests before Congress.

Options

When Congress considers appropriations or authorization for the department, it could take a number of different approaches to the DHS headquarters consolidation process. The following five examples of possible ways forward are discussed below:

- Termination and site disposal—choosing to invest no further funding in a DHS presence and not having them occupy the St. Elizabeths campus;

- Completion of Coast Guard Headquarters only—consolidating the Coast Guard headquarters on the St. Elizabeths campus, but not proceeding with the rest of the project;

- Coast Guard Headquarters, Operations Center and Management—consolidating the Coast Guard headquarters on the St. Elizabeths campus, and proceeding with the next phase;

- Rescoping Coast Guard Headquarters—using the new facility originally intended for the Coast Guard as the site of a rescoped DHS headquarters; and

- Expediting project completion—going beyond the existing funding request and taking steps to accelerate full consolidation.

Termination and Site Disposal

If Congress believes that consolidating DHS headquarters at St. Elizabeths is no longer appropriate, and that in light of that, consolidating Coast Guard headquarters in Anacostia would not have a beneficial effect, it could choose to cease funding for the project altogether and legislatively bar the Coast Guard from occupying the new building. If Congress were to pursue this option, and the proposed highway infrastructure project could be deferred.

Under this option, the Coast Guard would not move into its new facility, and would have to identify new headquarters facilities on an expedited basis. DHS headquarters functions would remain distributed across the National Capital Region. The department's headquarters would still

---

[81] The Partnership for Public Service, "The Best Places to Work in The Federal Government," 2011. Rankings for the Department of Homeland Security as downloaded from http://bestplacestowork.org/BPTW/rankings/detail/HS00 on May 15, 2012.

be heavily reliant on leased space for its real estate needs, which in addition to bearing higher costs than federally-owned space, would run counter to the government's stated preference to use federal owned space for national security real estate needs.

GSA would still need to maintain the St. Elizabeths campus until another use is identified for it and the nearly-completed building intended for the Coast Guard, or the property is disposed of. This would entail continued costs to GSA,[82] and disposal would be complicated by the St. Elizabeths' status as a National Historic Landmark, and the security concerns of the White House Communications Agency (WHCA), which has facilities overlooked by the St. Elizabeths campus. It seems highly unlikely the Federal government would recover its investment in the property.

Completion of Coast Guard Headquarters Only

Congress may not choose to invest further in the consolidated headquarters for DHS due to budget constraints or a desire for DHS to rethink the consolidated headquarters model. However, it may choose to fund completion and operational transition costs for the Coast Guard to occupy their portion of the facility, to ensure more of a return on the investment already made in the site than expected under the above-described termination option.

This would satisfy the Coast Guard's immediate needs for headquarters space, and provide operational benefits, as their new headquarters would be a single facility built expressly for them, as opposed to their current situation—multiple leased offices on different sites not built to their specifications.[83] However, it is worth noting that the campus would have been designed differently for the Coast Guard as a single tenant—shared facilities at the campus center would have been moved to the Coast Guard building to minimize the footprint, and costly upgrades to the campus utility infrastructure to support follow-on phases of the consolidation would not have been made. Capital costs would still be incurred to establish a new security perimeter for the scaled-down facility, but these would be significantly less than the costs of completing the St. Elizabeths project as envisioned. This option would bring the Coast Guard headquarters into compliance with GSA's practice of putting its secured areas for national security in federally owned facilities.

The more modern and capable facility could have positive impacts on the morale of the Coast Guard, although this could be balanced by perceptions of the new headquarters being isolated due to its location, which would not be near other DHS components or connected to other federal facilities. It could also have a negative impact on departmental cohesiveness, as the remainder of the department's headquarters functions would still remain at existing distributed facilities on short-term leases.

---

[82] Oral testimony of Robert Peck, Commissioner, Public Buildings Service, General Services Administration, "Review and Status of the Multibillion-Dollar Department of Homeland Security Relocation Project in Washington, DC, and its Impacts on the U.S. Coast Guard," House Transportation and Infrastructure Subcommittee on Coast Guard and Maritime Transportation, September 23, 2011. Available at http://www.gpo.gov/fdsys/pkg/CHRG-112hhrg68482/pdf/CHRG-112hhrg68482.pdf.

[83] Oral testimony of VADM John Currier (USCG), Deputy Commandant for Mission Support, "Review and Status of the Multibillion-Dollar Department of Homeland Security Relocation Project in Washington, DC, and its Impacts on the U.S. Coast Guard," House Transportation and Infrastructure Subcommittee on Coast Guard and Maritime Transportation, September 23, 2011. Available at http://www.gpo.gov/fdsys/pkg/CHRG-112hhrg68482/pdf/CHRG-112hhrg68482.pdf.

The proposed highway infrastructure project could be deferred, as it is needed to address anticipated traffic volume from later phases of the project. GSA would still need to maintain portions of the St. Elizabeths campus until another use for the remaining property is identified, or the property is disposed of. As in the termination scenario, this would entail continued costs to GSA, and disposal would be complicated by the status of St. Elizabeths as a historic property. Security concerns of WHCA would be mitigated somewhat by the presence of the Coast Guard on part of the property, although the interim fence line providing security for the Coast Guard headquarters would not encompass all potentially sensitive areas of the property.

Coast Guard Headquarters, Operations Center, and Management

If Congress chooses to support further DHS consolidation at St. Elizabeths, including the post-Katrina recommendation to establish a more capable department-wide operations center, but not fund the remainder of the project as envisioned due to budget constraints, it could choose to go beyond the above scenario. The next step would be to provide additional funding for completion of the departmental operations center and the renovation of the necessary buildings to relocate the executive-level departmental management to the St. Elizabeths campus.

This would address the single operational concern raised repeatedly by Admiral Allen—namely, the lack of the department-wide operations center. While funding the reuse of the existing historical buildings to house the Secretary's offices would represent a significant investment and would not generate all the management efficiencies of the original project, this alternative could allow for further consolidation to be reconsidered and funded at a future time. It would also leverage part of the investment that has been made in campus infrastructure. Increasing the number of personnel at the site would increase the need to improve the surrounding highway system.

In terms of the cultural impact on the department, this option could show continuing progress toward a more fully integrated DHS, although the end point of the project would remain unclear. Given the evolving nature of best workplace practices, including increasing use of telecommuting and shared office spaces, this could provide useful flexibility should DHS wish to significantly revise its plan.

Rescoping Coast Guard Headquarters to House Other Elements

Congress could attempt to capture some of the benefits of headquarters consolidation with a smaller up-front investment by mandating a reconfiguring of the Coast Guard headquarters as an ad hoc departmental headquarters space. Under this scenario, the DHS Secretary's office would occupy part of the newly constructed space as would a departmental operations center. This would provide a limited operational benefit—the 1.2 million square feet of space Coast Guard headquarters will provide is newer, but with roughly the same overall space as the NAC—but at the cost of disrupting Coast Guard headquarters functions that would remain divided, rather than consolidated, and further delaying occupancy of the headquarters.

Given the limitations of trying to repurpose the already designed and constructed Coast Guard space, it may well not be possible to establish a more robust departmental operations center than already exists at the NAC for DHS under this scenario. Ceasing development of the consolidated Coast Guard headquarters would deny the Coast Guard the operational benefits of their own consolidated headquarters and could undermine the component's morale.

Expediting Project Completion

Congress could also choose to make this project a higher priority among those in the discretionary budget and fund this project aggressively, in an attempt to expedite its completion and salvage whatever savings are possible from coordinated construction of the remaining elements.

This option would provide the maximum operational return, providing the infrastructure requested by DHS in its plans for a consolidated headquarters. As such, if seen to completion, pursuing this option could help reduce barriers to information flow, support coordinated planning and promote the development of a "One DHS" culture. There is a question as to whether the department's six year old plans still adequately reflect the needs of present-day DHS, given the changes in the DHS budget and changing workplace practices (such as the growth of telework).

It is difficult to assess the precise budgetary impact of this option, as the Administration has indicated they are developing a new construction schedule and revised cost estimate. However, it would clearly require a significant adjustment of priorities across the federal discretionary budget to make room in the DHS and GSA allocations for a level of investment significantly higher than what has been provided since FY2009. While this option could capitalize on some savings from coordinated construction, many of those savings are no longer available.

Pursuit of this option could be interpreted as a statement that the general DHS structure is a settled matter for Congress and could provide the benefits outlined in DHS's justifications for this project. However, there is no guarantee of improved departmental performance or enhanced morale with this or any of these options.

Conclusion

In can be argued that the creation of DHS was a reaction to a national crisis. After years of reaction, departmental reorganization, and increasing distance from the events that led to the creation of the department, there are issues that remain from that more tumultuous time that have yet to be addressed.[84] The consolidation of DHS headquarters functions is one of those unresolved issues. Congress and the department are operating in a different environment than when the consolidation plan was originally drawn up, both in terms of the security threats the nation faces and the budgetary situation. The Administration's new proposal for St. Elizabeths may fit these new realities better than the existing plan.

It is worth noting that any option Congress chooses—even an option to not make a decision on the long-term fate of the project—will bear significant costs. The costs manifest themselves as construction and move costs for a consolidated headquarters, continued rents for leases across the National Capital Region for maintaining existing headquarters facilities, or the possible (and more difficult to quantify) security, management, communications, logistics, and command and control impacts presented by both the status quo or any proposed change. Given the size of the department and the importance of its missions, how the DHS headquarters functions are housed and managed will be an issue of congressional interest for years to come.

---

[84] "The Department of Homeland Security: Past, Present and Future," Panel Discussion at the Aspen Security Forum, July 27, 2012. Video available at http://aspensecurityforum.org/2012-video-day-3.

Appendix. History of Project Appropriations

Analysis of Fiscal Years with Denied Requests or Partial Funding

Appropriations for the DHS headquarters consolidation effort are carried in two bills: the construction needs for the basic buildings and infrastructure are typically funded in the Financial Services and General Government appropriations bill, through the General Services Administration (GSA), while the mission-specific needs are typically funded through the Homeland Security appropriations bill. **Table A-1** at the end of the appendix provides a summary of funding requested and ultimately appropriated for the consolidation of Coast Guard and DHS headquarters at St. Elizabeths.

FY2007

In the course of developing the FY2007 appropriations bills, the House Appropriations Subcommittee for Homeland Security stated that the initial proposal for Coast Guard headquarters evolved into a consolidated headquarters project without answers being provided to the committee on the reasoning behind the site choice, the full range of costs involved and what components would move. The Committee rejected funding for the Coast Guard Headquarters project in the report accompanying the bill.[85] Roughly a month later, the Senate Homeland Security appropriations report took a substantively similar position, which was echoed in the final conference report. Both House and Senate appropriators were concerned that DHS was wasting money on investing in the Nebraska Avenue Complex, which they would then abandon for a newer, larger, more expensive headquarters at St. Elizabeths.[86]

When the House Appropriations Committee reported out the Transportation, Treasury and Housing and Urban Development appropriations bill, which at the time included GSA, the committee report for the bill also rejected the Coast Guard project, but on the basis of their belief that the project would have little positive impact on the local community.[87] The Senate companion report was silent on the project, and the year ending continuing resolution (P.L. 110-5) expressly denied funding for a Coast Guard Headquarters at St. Elizabeths.[88]

FY2008

For FY2008, the House Appropriations Committee recommended partial funding for the project, while still expressing concerns about overinvesting in the Nebraska Avenue Complex and the breadth of the St. Elizabeths project.[89] The Senate also provided partial funding for the project, but in the Consolidated Appropriations Act, 2008 (P.L. 110-161), $6 million was provided for continuing improvements at the Nebraska Avenue Complex, rather than the $101 million

---

[85] U.S. Congress, House Committee on Appropriations, Subcommittee on Homeland Security, *Department of Homeland Security Appropriations Bill, 2007*, Report together with Additional Views to accompany H.R. 5441, 109th Cong., 2nd sess., May 22, 2006, H.Rept. 109-476 (Washington: GPO, 2006), pp. 15-16.

[86] H.Rept. 109-699, pp. 118-119.

[87] H.Rept. 109-495, p. 175.

[88] P.L. 110-5, *Revised Continuing Appropriations Resolution*, 121 Stat. 57.

[89] H.Rept. 110-181, p. 18-19.

provided in the House bill for the NAC and St. Elizabeths or the $88 million provided in the Senate for St. Elizabeths alone.[90]

In FY2008, the GSA appropriations were moved to the Financial Services and General Government Appropriations Act, where they remain today. The House Financial Services Appropriations Subcommittee expressed concern about the size of the Coast Guard project, and about possible overinvestment in the NAC given the impending move, but did not explicitly restrict funding for the projects, despite undesignated cuts to the accounts that would support the projects.[91] The Senate funded the requested projects in full, but in the final version of P.L. 110-161, only $28 million in funding for the NAC remained.[92]

FY2011

No request was made for the St. Elizabeths project for FY2010 through either GSA or DHS. In FY2011, the requested budget for the project was unmet, falling over half a billion dollars short of the combined request, despite testimony before the House Appropriations Committee's Homeland Security Subcommittee about the urgency of the need and the potential long-term budget savings.[93] FY2011 appropriations for federal government operations were provided through a year-long CR, which included $77 million for the headquarters consolidation project through DHS.[94] The GSA had requested $381 million for St. Elizabeths, ultimately provided $30 million to the project from the $82 million it received for construction projects nationwide under the CR.[95]

FY2012

For FY2012, the Administration requested $215 million for headquarters consolidation through the DHS budget, including $160 million for new construction at St. Elizabeths, and $55 million for lease consolidation. They also requested $217 million in the General Services Administration budget for the project through the Federal Buildings Fund, including funding for planned highway alterations to provide better motor vehicle access to the campus.

The House did not fund the project in the House-passed DHS appropriations bill. In report language, the Committee stated:

> …[B]oth costs and schedule of the current project are matters of concern for the Committee. In hearings the Committee held on the St. Elizabeths project in 2010, it became clear that adequate cost controls were essential for this project … Yet costs have grown in a year from $3,400,000,000 to $3,600,000,000 chiefly due to increases in the General Services

---

[90] House Appropriations Committee Print, *Consolidated Appropriations Act, 2008* (P.L. 110-161), *Division E—Department of Homeland Security Appropriations Act, 2008*, p. 1022.

[91] H.Rept. 110-207, p. 63-64.

[92] P.L. 110-161, *Division D—Financial Services and General Government Appropriations Act, 2008*, p. 828.

[93] U.S. Congress, House Committee on Appropriations, Subcommittee on Homeland Security, *Hearings, Part 2*, Homeland Security Headquarters Facilities, 111th Cong., 2nd sess., March 25, 2010 (Washington: GPO, 2010), pp. 333-405.

[94] P.L. 112-10, 125 Stat. 140.

[95] Department of Homeland Security, "DHS Headquarters Consolidation: CRS St. Elizabeths Tour" slide deck, November 16, 2011, p. 7.

Administration share of the project. The Committee notes that dependence on GSA funding requires coordination of funding and management, and that the proposed DHS request, even if resources were available, would likely not coincide with necessary GSA funding. Furthermore, delays are already being factored into the Department's planning, as it has projected it will postpone work on the FEMA section of the facility.[96]

In minority views included in the report, the ranking members of the House subcommittee and full committee had a different perspective:

> Of particular concern is the decision to provide no funding for the new DHS headquarters or for the consolidation of leased property, a penny-wise and pound-foolish decision. Already, based on the delay in finalizing the 2011 bill and the reduced resources provided in that bill for DHS headquarters construction activities, the cost of the headquarters project has grown by $200 million, from a total cost of $3.4 billion to $3.6 billion. The decision to deny an additional $159,643,000 in 2012 to finalize construction of the first phase of the new headquarters project and begin construction on the second phase will result in higher costs in the out years and will delay, by at least one year, when the Coast Guard can move into its new headquarters facility (phase one), which is already under construction.[97]

The Senate Appropriations Committee recommended $56 million in Title V of their version of the DHS appropriations bill to complete the Coast Guard headquarters facility, $159 million (74%) below the President's requested funding level. The Senate Appropriations Committee also expressed concern that limited funding would result in no other DHS headquarters components using the St. Elizabeths campus, and included in their bill a requirement that DHS provide within 60 days of enactment an expenditure plan and an initial analysis of the mix of offices to be housed at the headquarters complex.[98]

The House Appropriations Committee's Financial Services Subcommittee rejected the Administration's entire $840 million request for construction and acquisition under GSA's Federal Buildings Fund. In zeroing out the request for construction, the report noted "Adding to the Federal inventory of buildings is not welcomed at a time when the management and use of the current inventory is less than optimal."[99] The chairmen of the House subcommittee and full committee expressed concern about the deep cuts in GSA's budget, noting that it reversed a position taken by the current chamber majority in the FY2008 bill. However, the report does not mention the DHS project specifically.

The Senate Appropriations Committee's Financial Services Subcommittee provided $65 million for the entire construction and acquisition activity at GSA, rather than the $840 million requested. No mention is made in the bill or report of the DHS headquarters project.[100]

In the final consolidated appropriations bill for FY2012, the overall combined request of $377 million for GSA and DHS contributions to St. Elizabeths resulted in only $93 million in

---

[96] H.Rept. 112-91, p. 16.

[97] Ibid., p. 202.

[98] S.Rept. 112-74, pp. 161-162.

[99] U.S. Congress, House Committee on Appropriations, Subcommittee on Financial Services and General Government, *Financial Services and General Government Appropriations Bill, 2012*, Report to accompany H.R. 2434, 112th Cong., 1st sess., July 7, 2011, H.Rept. 112-136 (Washington: GPO, 2011), pp. 48-49.

[100] The Senate Appropriations Committee Financial Services Subcommittee provided $65 million for the entire construction and acquisition activity at GSA, rather than the $840 million requested

appropriations, with $56 million provided to DHS to complete only the construction of the Coast Guard portion of the headquarters.[101] The remaining $37 million for the St. Elizabeths project came from the $50 million GSA received for construction projects nationwide. DHS has indicated that the GSA funding was inadequate to complete work as planned for the Coast Guard to occupy its new headquarters, so several elements of Phase I have been delayed and the funding for those elements redirected to ensure the needed work could be done.

Table A-1. DHS and GSA Appropriations for St. Elizabeths (FY2006-FY2012)

(in thousands of dollars of budget authority)

FY	Dept.	Activity	Request	Appropriation
	GSA	Coast Guard Consolidation	24,900	24,900
2006	GSA	St. Elizabeths West Campus Infrastructure	13,095	13,095
		Total	**37,995**	**37,995**
	GSA	Coast Guard Consolidation	306,139	0
	GSA	St. Elizabeths West Campus Infrastructure	6,444	6,444
2007		*GSA Subtotal*	*312,583*	*6,444*
	DHS	Coast Guard Headquarters (Operating Expenses)	50,200	0
		Total	**356,339**	**6,444**
	GSA	DHS Consolidation and Development of St. Elizabeths Campus	318,887	0
	GSA	St. Elizabeths West Campus Infrastructure	20,752	0
2008	GSA	St. Elizabeths West Campus Site Acquisition	7,000	0
		GSA Subtotal	*346,639*	*0*
	DHS	Consolidated Headquarters at St. Elizabeths	120,000	0
		Total	**466,639**	**0**
	GSA	DHS Consolidation and Development of St. Elizabeths Campus	331,390	331,390
	GSA	St. Elizabeths West Campus Infrastructure	8,249	8,249
2009	GSA	St. Elizabeths West Campus Site Acquisition	7,000	7,000
		GSA Subtotal	*346,639*	*346,639*
	DHS	Coast Guard/DHS Headquarters	120,000	97,578
		Total	**466,639**	**444,217**
	GSA	Consolidated Headquarters at St. Elizabeths	n/a	450,000
2009 (ARRA)	DHS	Consolidated Headquarters at St. Elizabeths	n/a	200,000
		Total ARRA funds	**—**	**650,000**
2010		No Request	—	—
2011	GSA	St. Elizabeths DHS Consolidation and Development	267,675	30,000

[101] In their spending plan released on January 27, 2012, GSA indicated they would spend $37 million on the St. Elizabeths project.

FY	Dept.	Activity	Request	Appropriation
	GSA	St. Elizabeths West Campus Infrastructure	99,281	0
	GSA	St. Elizabeths Historic Preservation Mitigation	4,990	0
	GSA	St, Elizabeths Highway Interchange	8,350	0
		GSA Subtotal	*380,296*	*30,000*
	DHS	Consolidated Headquarters at St. Elizabeths	287,800	77,245
		Total	**668,096**	**107,245**
	GSA	St. Elizabeths Activities	100,000	0
	GSA	St. Elizabeths East Campus Road Development	20,400	0
	GSA	St. Elizabeths Highway Interchange	55,400	0
2012	GSA	St. Elizabeths West Campus Infrastructure	41,906	37,300
		GSA Subtotal	*217,706*	*37,300*
	DHS	Consolidated Headquarters at St. Elizabeths	159,643	55,979
		Total	**377,349**	**93,279**

Source: CRS analysis of GSA and DHS budget request documents and appropriations conference reports.

Notes: GSA funding for headquarters consolidation and St. Elizabeth has been provided under multiple project names over the course of the project. Subtotals are therefore included in the table for GSA. In FY2007, funding for Coast Guard Headquarters consolidation was requested under Coast Guard Operating Expenses, Headquarters Directorates. GSA provided $30 million in FY2011, designated for critical occupancy issues for the Coast Guard and the first stages of the Departmental Operations Center. It was not attributed to specific projects.

Author Contact Information

William L. Painter
Analyst in Emergency Management and Homeland
Security Policy
wpainter@crs.loc.gov, 7-3335